London

by Jessica Rudolph

Consultant: Karla Ruiz, MA
Teachers College, Columbia University
New York, New York

BEARPORT
PUBLISHING

New York, New York

Credits

Cover, © Salparaclis/Shutterstock; 2–3, © Kamira/Shutterstock; TOC Top, © Christopher Elwell/
Dreamstime; 4–5, © QQ7/Shutterstock; 7, © Claudio Divizia/Shutterstock; 8L, © Millionstock.
com/Shutterstock; 8–9, © Ewelina Wachala/Shutterstock; 9R, © Intoit/Dreamstime; 10, © Kiev.
Victor/Shutterstock; 11, © majaiva/iStock; 12T, © r.nagy/Shutterstock; 12B, © giorgiogalano/iStock;
13, © Christian Mueller/Shutterstock; 14, © ileana_bt/Shutterstock; 15, © Marco Prati/Shutterstock;
16, © Ron Ellis/Shutterstock; 17T, © Bob Masters/Alamy Stock Photo; 17B, © Claudio Divizia/Shutterstock;
18, © DronG/Shutterstock; 19, © Stolyevych Yuliya/Shutterstock; 20, © Dmitry Naumov/Shutterstock;
21T, © Chris Dorney/Dreamstime; 21, Public Domain; 22 (Clockwise from TR), © Moomusician/
Shutterstock, © Kiev.Victor/Shutterstock, © Alexander Chaikin/Shutterstock, © Ron Ellis/Shutterstock,
and © William Perugini/Shutterstock; 23 (T to B), © antoniodiaz/Shutterstock, Public Domain, © Flik47/
Shutterstock, © cobraphotography/Shutterstock, Public Domian, and © Monkey Business Images/
Shutterstock; 24, © PHOTOCREO Michal Bednarek/Shutterstock.

Publisher: Kenn Goin
Editor: J. Clark
Creative Director: Spencer Brinker
Photo Researcher: Thomas Persano

Library of Congress Cataloging-in-Publication Data

Names: Rudolph, Jessica, author.
Title: London / by Jessica Rudolph.
Description: New York, New York : Bearport Publishing, 2018. | Series:
  Citified! | Ages 5 to 8. | Includes bibliographical references and index.
Identifiers: LCCN 2017007439 (print) | LCCN 2017007896 (ebook) | ISBN
  9781684022328 (library bound) | ISBN 9781684022861 (ebook)
Subjects: LCSH: London (England)—Juvenile literature.
Classification: LCC DA678 .R77 2018 (print) | LCC DA678 (ebook) | DDC
  942.1—dc23
LC record available at https://lccn.loc.gov/2017007439

For more information, write to Bearport Publishing Company, Inc.,
45 West 21st Street, Suite 3B, New York, New York 10010. Printed in the
United States of America.

10 9 8 7 6 5 4 3 2 1

Contents

Welcome to

LONDON

The Capital of the United Kingdom!

About 18 million people from overseas visit London each year.

London is not just the **capital** of the United Kingdom.

It's also the largest city.

More than eight million people live there!

London is also the capital of England, which is one of the countries in the United Kingdom.

Scotland

Northern Ireland

England

London

Wales

Buckingham Palace is one of the homes of the English **monarchs**.

You can tour parts of the palace.

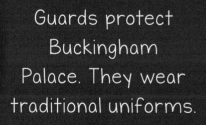

Guards protect Buckingham Palace. They wear traditional uniforms.

Queen Elizabeth II, the current monarch

Take a ride on the London Eye!

It's located along the Thames (TEMZ) River.

You can walk inside the capsules that go around and around.

capsule

On a clear day, you can see for 25 miles (40 km) from the top of the London Eye.

Stroll down busy Portobello Road for some shopping.

The Royal Borough of Kensington and Chelsea PORTOBELLO ROAD, W. 11.

Clothes, food, jewelry, and other products are sold in stalls and shops.

Customers on Portobello Road can often **bargain** with shop owners for lower prices.

There are lots of fun museums for kids to visit in London.

Gaze at giant dinosaur bones at the Natural History Museum!

Roar!

At the London Science Museum, children can learn how astronauts walked on the moon.

Don't miss out on Shakespeare's Globe.

This building is a **reconstruction** of the theater where William Shakespeare put on plays 400 years ago.

Today, people can watch performances of his plays at the Globe.

THERE IS NO DARKNESS BUT IGNORANCE

Shakespeare lived from 1564 to 1616. He wrote plays such as *Macbeth* and *Romeo and Juliet.*

Try some English food at a London restaurant—like fish and chips!

Chips is another name for French fries.

One tasty English dessert is called Eton mess. It's made with strawberries, **meringue**, and cream.

The Tower of London has a long history.

It's been a prison, a home to kings, and a site of **beheadings**!

Today, guides take visitors on tours of the building.

tour guide

In 1536, King Henry VIII had his wife Anne Boleyn beheaded at the Tower of London!

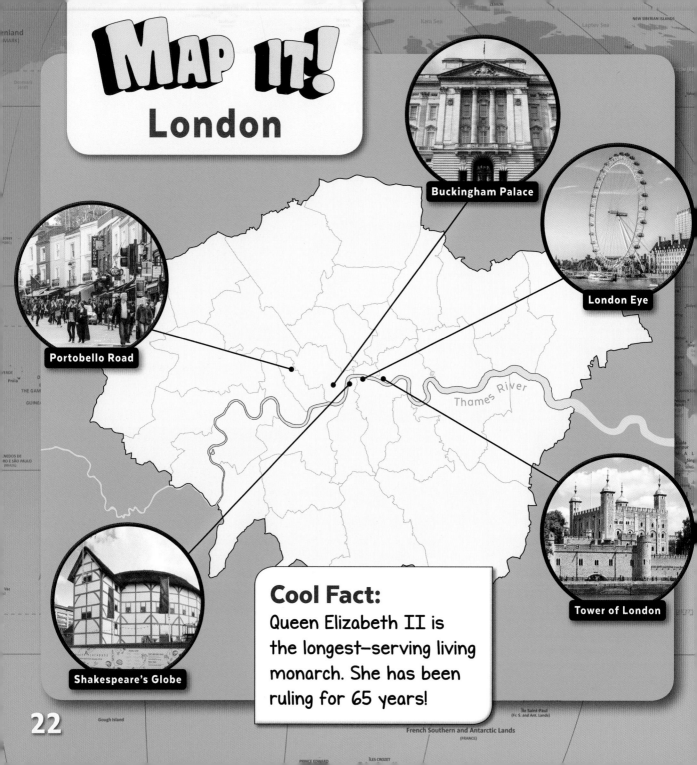

MAP IT!
London

Buckingham Palace

London Eye

Portobello Road

Thames River

Tower of London

Shakespeare's Globe

Cool Fact:
Queen Elizabeth II is the longest-serving living monarch. She has been ruling for 65 years!

bargain (BAR-gin) to talk over the terms of a purchase

beheadings (bih-HED-ingz) events where people's heads were chopped off

capital (KAP-uh-tuhl) the city where a country's government is based

meringue (muh-RANG) a mixture of beaten egg whites and sugar on cakes, pies, and other sweets

monarchs (MAHN-arks) leaders who inherit their positions and rule for life

reconstruction (ree-kuhn-STRUK-shuhn) something that has been put back to its original state

Index

Read More

Butterfield, Moira. *London: City Trails (Lonely Planet Kids).* Oakland, CA: Lonely Planet (2016).

Rubbino, Salvatore. *A Walk In London.* Somerville, MA: Candlewick Press (2011).

Learn More Online

To learn more about London, visit
www.bearportpublishing.com/Citified

About the Author

Jessica Rudolph lives in Connecticut.
She has edited and written many books
about history, science, and nature for children.